ENTREPRENEURSHIP UNLOCKED , FROM IDEA TO EMPIRE

JAZZ GANGWANI

Made with ♥ on the Notion Press Platform
www.notionpress.com

To the dreamers, the risk-takers, and the relentless doers—
those who dare to turn ideas into impact.

This book is dedicated to:

My family, who taught me resilience and believed in my
vision even when it seemed impossible.

My mentors, whose wisdom lit the path when I stumbled
in the dark.

Every aspiring entrepreneur, whose courage to begin fuels
the future of innovation.

"To caffeine, chaos, and the 3 AM breakthroughs—thank
you for keeping me company."

Special thanks to those who stood by me through late
nights, wild ideas, and the rollercoaster of
entrepreneurship.

Opportunities don't happen. You create them."
— Chris Grosser

Author :- *Jazz Gangwani*

Published by *NG.Publications.com*

May these pages empower you to build, fail, rise, and leave
a legacy.

Contents

Contents

FOREWORD

Entrepreneurship is not for the faint of heart. It's a journey of grit, resilience, and relentless curiosity—a path where uncertainty is the only certainty. Yet, it's also the most rewarding adventure you'll ever undertake.

When Jazz Gangwani first shared the vision for this book, I was struck by its clarity and practicality. Unlike many guides that romanticize entrepreneurship or drown readers in theory, [Insert Book Title] cuts through the noise. Jazz's approach is rooted in real-world experience, hard-won lessons, and actionable strategies that work for today's fast-paced, digital-first world.

I've spent decades mentoring founders, and I can confidently say this: The difference between those who succeed and those who stall isn't talent or luck—it's mindset, preparation, and the courage to act. In these pages, Jazz dismantles the myths holding aspiring entrepreneurs back and replaces them with frameworks you can apply immediately. Whether you're validating your first idea, navigating funding, or scaling a global brand, this book is your compass.

What makes this guide unique is its balance of inspiration and practicality. Jazz doesn't just tell you what to do; they show you how, with worksheets, case studies, and step-by-step blueprints. From Airbnb's humble beginnings to Tesla's audacious bets, the stories here remind us that every empire starts with a single step.

To the reader: Entrepreneurship is not about having all the answers. It's about asking the right questions, embracing the journey, and persisting when others quit. Let this book be your mentor, your cheerleader, and your roadmap. The world needs your ideas—now go build something extraordinary.

Published by ***NG.Publications.com***

PREFACE

The entrepreneurial journey is not a straight line—it's a wild, unpredictable adventure filled with detours, roadblocks, and moments of pure magic. This book was born from my own messy, exhilarating, and often humbling experiences as a founder. It's the guide I wish I'd had when I first stumbled into entrepreneurship, unsure of where to start or how to survive the inevitable storms.

When I launched my first business at [age/year], I made every mistake imaginable. I overcomplicated ideas, underestimated cash flow, and let self-doubt sabotage opportunities. But with each failure, I learned. With each pivot, I grew. Over time, I discovered patterns—principles that separated thriving entrepreneurs from those who burned out. This book distills those lessons into actionable steps, cutting through the noise to focus on what truly matters.

Why This Book?

Today's entrepreneurial landscape is both thrilling and overwhelming. Digital tools have democratized access, but they've also created endless distractions. Social media glorifies "overnight success," while ignoring the years of grind behind it. I wrote this guide to bridge that gap—to offer a realistic, no-fluff roadmap for building a business that lasts.

You'll find no theoretical jargon here. Instead, you'll get:

Practical frameworks (like the Lean Canvas and 90-Day Validation Sprint).

Raw stories of triumph and failure—from my own ventures to icons like Sara Blakely and Brian Chesky.

Worksheets and checklists to turn ideas into action, one page at a time.

Who Is This For?

This book is for the dreamers who've been called "unrealistic," the side hustlers ready to go all-in, and the seasoned founders seeking fresh strategies. Whether you're a student with a dorm-room idea or a corporate escapee craving freedom, these pages meet you where you are.

A Note on Mindset

Entrepreneurship is as much about psychology as it is about strategy. That's why I've woven mindset principles into every chapter. Success isn't just about what you do—it's about how you think.

Gratitude

To my readers: Thank you for trusting me with your time and ambition. Entrepreneurship is a team sport, and I'm honored to be part of your squad. If this book helps one person avoid a pitfall or seize an opportunity, I'll consider it a win.

Now, let's roll up our sleeves and begin. The world needs your ideas.

Jazz Gangwani
Published by NG.Publications.com

ACKNOWLEDGEMENTS

Writing this book has been a journey of collaboration, and I owe immense thanks to the many people who made it possible.

To the NG.Publications Team:
Your expertise, patience, and belief in this project turned a raw manuscript into a polished guide. Thank you for championing this book and guiding me through every step—from brainstorming to launch.

To My Family:
Mom and Dad, your unwavering support gave me the courage to leap into entrepreneurship. [Partner/Kids/Siblings], thank you for enduring my late-night writing sessions and chaotic deadlines. This book exists because you believed in me long before I did.

To My Mentors and Advisors:
[Name(s)], your wisdom shaped my entrepreneurial journey. Thank you for answering frantic calls, challenging my assumptions, and reminding me that failure is just feedback.

To the Beta Readers and Early Supporters:
Your honest feedback sharpened every chapter. Special thanks to [Name/Group] for testing exercises, flagging typos, and asking the tough questions.

To My Friends and Cheerleaders:
[Name(s)], you kept me sane with coffee runs, pep talks, and much-needed distractions. Entrepreneurship can be lonely—you made it a shared adventure.

To the Entrepreneurial Community:
To the founders who shared their stories, the podcast hosts who amplified my voice, and the strangers who inspired

me with their grit—this book is a tribute to your collective spirit.

To You, the Reader:

Thank you for trusting me with your time and ambition. If these pages spark even one idea or save you a misstep, my mission is complete.

"If I have seen further, it is by standing on the shoulders of giants."

— Isaac Newton

With gratitude,

Jazz Gangwani

Published by **NG.Publications.com**

PROLOGUE

The Journey Begins Here

Every great adventure starts with a single step—often into the unknown.

It was 3 AM on a Tuesday when I sat hunched over my laptop, surrounded by empty coffee cups and crumpled sticky notes. My first startup, a fledgling app designed to simplify grocery shopping, had just crashed. Not metaphorically—literally. The servers were down, investors were furious, and my savings account screamed "abort mission." In that moment, I felt the weight of every entrepreneur's darkest fear: What if I'm not cut out for this?

But here's the truth I wish someone had told me then: Entrepreneurship isn't about avoiding failure. It's about learning to dance in the storm.

This book is not a collection of success stories polished for Instagram. It's a raw, honest map of the entrepreneurial wilderness—the peaks of triumph, the valleys of doubt, and the hidden trails that lead to breakthroughs. Whether you're a student scribbling ideas in a notebook, a corporate refugee craving autonomy, or a side hustler ready to go all-in, this journey is for you.

The World Needs Disruptors

Think of the Airbnb founders renting air mattresses in their living room, or Sara Blakely selling fax machines door-to-door to fund Spanx. They didn't start with perfect plans or Silicon Valley connections. They started with a problem, a spark of curiosity, and the audacity to try.

In these pages, you'll discover:

Why mindset matters more than money.

How to turn failure into fuel.

The systems that scale ideas into empires.

But this isn't just a book—it's a call to action. The tools, frameworks, and stories here are your compass. The rest? That's up to you.

A Note on Courage

Entrepreneurship is not for the fearless. It's for the courageous—those who move forward even when their knees shake. You'll make mistakes. You'll doubt yourself. You'll want to quit. But if you persist, you'll also experience moments of pure magic: the first sale, the loyal customer, the team that feels like family.

So, take a deep breath. Turn the page. Let's begin.

"The only way to do great work is to love what you do."
— Steve Jobs

Jazz Gangwani
Published by ***NG.Publications.com***

TABLE OF CONTENT

I
What Is Entrepreneurship?

1.1 Definition and Core Principles
Entrepreneurship is the art of identifying opportunities, mobilizing resources, and creating value in the face of uncertainty. It's not just about starting a business—it's about solving problems that matter.

Key Principles:

Value Creation: Focus on solving pain points (e.g., Slack simplifying team communication).

Resourcefulness: The "Jugaad" mindset (Indian philosophy of frugal innovation).

Ownership: Entrepreneurs bear risks but also reap rewards (e.g., Jeff Bezos risking Amazon's early profits on AWS).

1.2 Historical Evolution

Ancient Trade (3000 BCE): Mesopotamian merchants trading grains and textiles.

Medieval Guilds (1200s): Craftsmen forming alliances to protect trade secrets.

20th-Century Innovators: Henry Ford's assembly line revolutionizing manufacturing.

Digital Age (2000s): Mark Zuckerberg turning a dorm-room project into Meta.

1.3 Types of Entrepreneurs

Type Focus Example

Small Business Local impact,stability Family-owned grocery store

Scalable Startup Disruption, rapid growth Tesla, Airbnb

Social Entrepreneur Societal change Grameen Bank (microfinance)

Lifestyle Flexibility, passion Travel bloggers

1.4 Why Entrepreneurship Matters

Economic Impact: Startups account for 44% of U.S. economic activity.

Innovation: 75% of Fortune 500 companies began as small ventures.

Global Trends: Remote work, AI, and sustainability are reshaping industries.

1.5 Case Study: Spanx by Sara Blakely

Problem: Women's undergarments were uncomfortable and unflattering.

Solution: Invented footless pantyhose with no visible seams.

Outcome: $1.2B valuation with no external funding.

Lesson: "Don't let inexperience stop you—use it to think differently."

1.6 Worksheet:

List 3 societal trends (e.g., AI, sustainability). How could they inspire your business?

II
The Entrepreneurial Mindset

2.1 Core Traits

Resilience:

Science: Neuroplasticity—how the brain adapts to challenges.

Example: Oprah Winfrey overcoming poverty and discrimination.

Exercise: Write a "Failure Résumé" listing lessons from past setbacks.

Adaptability:

Framework: OODA Loop (Observe, Orient, Decide, Act).

Case Study: Nintendo pivoting from playing cards to video games.

Risk Tolerance:

Tool: Risk Matrix (plot likelihood vs. impact).

2.2 Psychological Foundations

Growth Mindset (Carol Dweck): Belief that abilities can be developed.

Grit (Angela Duckworth): Perseverance for long-term goals.

2.3 Daily Habits of Top Entrepreneurs

Morning Routine:

Tim Cook (Apple): 4 AM emails, gym, mindfulness.

Arianna Huffington: Sleep prioritization, no phones in bed.

Evening Routine:

Bill Gates: Reflect on daily learnings via journaling.

2.4 Case Study: Elon Musk

Mindset Strategies:

First Principles Thinking: Breaking problems into fundamentals (e.g., SpaceX reducing rocket costs).

Quote: "If something is important enough, you do it even if the odds are against you."

2.5 Worksheet:

Self-Assessment: Rate your mindset traits (1–10) and create an improvement plan.

2.6 Template: Weekly Resilience Tracker

Day Challenge Faced Lesson Learned
Monday Rejected pitch Refine messaging

III

Finding a Profitable Business Idea

3.1 Idea Generation Frameworks

SCAMPER:

Substitute, Combine, Adapt, Modify, Put to another use, Eliminate, Reverse.

Example: Uber combined taxis with smartphone apps.

Jobs-To-Be-Done (JTBD):

Focus on the "job" customers hire your product to do (e.g., Starbucks sells "third place" experiences).

3.2 Trend Analysis

Tools:

Exploding Topics (trend discovery).

Google Keyword Planner (search volume analysis).
2024 Trends:
AI-driven healthcare, sustainable fashion, Web3 tools.

3.3 Validation Techniques

Pretotyping: Test demand before building (e.g., fake landing page with a "Buy Now" button).

Crowdfunding: Use Kickstarter to gauge interest (e.g., Pebble Smartwatch).

3.4 Case Study: Dropbox

Problem: File-sharing was clunky in 2007.

Validation: Launched a demo video that went viral, attracting 75,000 sign-ups overnight.

Lesson: "Build something people want, not just what you think is cool."

3.5 Worksheet:

Idea Scorecard:
   Market Demand: /5
   Competition: /5
   Your Expertise: /5

IV
Conducting Market Research

4.1 Types of Market Research

Primary Research:

Surveys: Use tools like SurveyMonkey or Google Forms to ask targeted questions (e.g., "What's your biggest challenge with fitness apps?").

Focus Groups: Gather 6–10 people for in-depth discussions (record sessions for insights).

Ethnographic Research: Observe customers in real-world settings (e.g., how shoppers navigate a store).

Secondary Research:

Industry Reports: Source data from IBISWorld, Statista, or Pew Research.

Competitor Analysis: Study Amazon reviews, social media comments, and pricing strategies of rivals.

4.2 Advanced Techniques

Sentiment Analysis: Use AI tools (e.g., Brandwatch) to analyze social media sentiment.

Cohort Analysis: Track customer behavior over time (e.g., repeat purchase rates).

4.3 Case Study: Dollar Shave Club

Research Insight: Men hated overpaying for razors and shopping in-store.

Action: Launched a subscription model with humorous YouTube ads.

Result: Acquired by Unilever for $1B.4

4.4 Worksheet:

Competitor SWOT Analysis:

CompetitorStrengthsWeaknessesOpportunitiesThreats

Brand XFast deliveryHigh pricesExpand to EuropeNew entrants

4.5 Template: Market Research Plan

1.Objective → 2. Methodology → 3. Timeline → 4. Budget.

V
Crafting a Solid Business Plan

5.1 Detailed Section Breakdown

Executive Summary:

Hook investors in 1–2 paragraphs (e.g., "Our AI tool reduces hiring bias by 40%").

Market Analysis:

Include TAM, SAM, SOM (Total, Serviceable, Obtainable Market).

Financial Projections:

3-year forecasts for revenue, expenses, and profit margins.

5.2 Common Mistakes to Avoid

Overestimating demand (use conservative estimates).

Ignoring competitor threats (address them head-on).

5.3 Case Study: Tesla's 2006 Master Plan

Phase 1: Build expensive sports car (Roadster) to fund R&D.

Phase 2: Use profits to create affordable models (Model 3).

Phase 3: Scale renewable energy solutions (SolarCity, Powerwall).

5.4 Worksheet:

Draft a One-Page Business Plan:

Problem → Solution → Target Market → Revenue Model.

5.5 Template: Financial Projection Spreadsheet

Year Revenue COGS Gross Profit

2024 $150K $60K $90K

VI

Funding Your Business

6.1 Funding Options Deep Dive

Bootstrapping:

Pros: Full control, no debt.

Cons: Slower growth.

Tool: Profit-first budgeting (allocate revenue to expenses, taxes, profit).

Venture Capital:

Term Sheet Clauses: Liquidation preferences, anti-dilution rights.

Pitch Tip: Highlight traction (e.g., "500 active users in 3 months").

6.2 Case Study: Oculus VR

Crowdfunding: Raised $2.4M on Kickstarter.

Exit: Sold to Facebook for $2B.

Lesson: Validate demand before scaling.

6.3 Worksheet:

Funding Needs Calculator:

Product Development (20K)+Marketing(20K)+Marketing(10K) + 6-Month Runway (30K)=**30K)=**60K Total**.

6.4 Template: Investor Pitch Deck Outline

1.Problem → 2. Solution → 3. Market Size → 4. Traction → 5. Team → 6. Ask.

VII
Legalizing Your Business

7.1 Step-by-Step Legal Setup

Choose a Structure:
    LLC: Best for small businesses (flexible taxes, asset protection).
    C-Corp: Ideal for venture-backed startups.
    Trademark Your Brand:
    Search USPTO.gov for existing trademarks.
    Compliance:
    GDPR (for EU customers), HIPAA (for health data).

7.2 Case Study: Uber's Regulatory Battles

Challenge: Banned in cities due to taxi union pressure.
    Solution: Lobbied for "ride-sharing" legislation.

7.3 Worksheet:

Legal Checklist:
    Business License
    EIN
    Insurance (General Liability)

7.4 Template: Non-Disclosure Agreement (NDA)

Parties → Confidential Info → Term → Exclusions.

VIII
Building Your Brand and Online Presence

8.1 Brand Identity Framework

Mission Statement: "To empower small businesses with affordable AI tools."
Voice and Tone: Friendly (Mailchimp) vs. Authoritative (IBM).

8.2 Website Optimization

SEO Basics:
Keyword research (Ahrefs, Ubersuggest).
Meta descriptions, alt text for images.
Conversion Tactics:

Clear CTAs ("Start Free Trial"), trust badges (SSL, testimonials).

8.3 Case Study: Glossier

Strategy: Built a cult following via Instagram UGC (user-generated content).
Tactic: Reposted customer selfies with #Glossier.
Result: $1.2B valuation.

8.4 Worksheet:

Social Media Audit:
Platform Followers Engagement Rate Top Post
Instagram 10K 4.2% Product launch reel

8.5 Template: Content Calendar

Date Platform Content Type Topic
11/1 TikTok Video "Day in the Life" vlog

IX

Selling and Marketing Your Product

9.1 Sales Funnel Optimization

TOFU (Top of Funnel):
Blog posts, YouTube tutorials, Pinterest pins.
MOFU (Middle of Funnel):
Email courses, free trials, webinars.
BOFU (Bottom of Funnel):
Limited-time discounts, case studies, live demos.

9.2 Psychology-Driven Marketing

Scarcity: "Only 3 seats left!"
Social Proof: Display testimonials with photos.

Reciprocity: Offer free tools or templates in exchange for emails.

9.3 Case Study: HubSpot

Inbound Marketing: Created free CRM tools to attract leads.
Result: $1.5B+ annual revenue.

9.4 Worksheet:

Customer Journey Map:
Awareness → Consideration → Purchase → Loyalty.

9.5 Template: Email Drip Campaign

1.Welcome Email → 2. Educational Content → 3. Soft Sell → 4. Hard Sell.

X

Growing and Scaling Your Business

10.1 Scaling Frameworks

Blitzscaling: Prioritize speed over efficiency (e.g., Uber in 2010s).

Sustainable Scaling: Gradual growth with profitability (e.g., Basecamp).

10.2 Automation Tools

Zapier: Connect apps (e.g., Gmail → Slack notifications).

ChatGPT: Automate customer support, content creation.

10.3 Case Study: Airbnb's Scaling Crisis

Problem: Trust issues between hosts and guests.
Solution: Introduced verified IDs, host guarantees, and reviews.

10.4 Worksheet:

Delegation Plan:
Tasks to Keep (CEO): Strategy, investor relations.
Tasks to Delegate (VA): Email management, scheduling.

10.5 Template: KPI Dashboard

Metric Target Actual
Monthly Revenue $50K $48K
Customer Churn 5% 7%

XI

Managing Finances and Budgeting

11.1 Financial Foundations for Startups

Budgeting Basics:

50/30/20 Rule: Allocate 50% to essentials, 30% to growth, 20% to emergencies.

Tools: QuickBooks for tracking, Excel for custom projections.

Cash Flow Management:

Forecasting: Predict 3–6 months of income/expenses (e.g., "If sales drop 20%, can we cover payroll?").

Burn Rate: Calculate monthly cash spent (e.g., 10K/month=6-monthrunwaywith10K/

month=6-monthrunwaywith60K savings).

11.2 Tax Strategies

Deductions: Home office (5% of rent), software subscriptions, marketing costs.

Quarterly Payments: Avoid penalties by estimating taxes (IRS Form 1040-ES).

11.3 Case Study: Mint.com

Strategy: Automated budgeting tools to simplify personal finance.
 Exit: Acquired by Intuit for $170M.
 Lesson: "Solve a universal pain point with intuitive tech."

11.4 Worksheet:

3-Month Cash Flow Projection:
 Month Revenue Expenses Net Profit
 Jan $20K $15K $5K

11.5 Template: Profit & Loss Statement

Category Amount
 Revenue $50K
 COGS $20K
 Gross Profit $30K

XII

Hiring and Building a Team

12.1 Hiring Strategies

First Hires: Prioritize revenue-generating roles (sales, marketing) or critical gaps (tech lead).

Remote Teams: Use Upwork for freelancers, Deel for global payroll compliance.

12.2 Building Culture

Core Values: Define 3–5 non-negotiables (e.g., "Customer First," "Radical Transparency").

Zappos Example: Paid $2K for employees to quit if they weren't aligned with culture.

12.3 Case Study: Netflix

Culture Code: "Freedom with Responsibility."
   Policy: No vacation tracking—focus on results.
   Result: 200M+ subscribers, $25B+ revenue

12.4 Worksheet:

Hiring Scorecard:
   RoleSkills NeededCultural Fit
   Sales LeadNegotiationCollaborative

12.5 Template: Job Posting Outline

1.Role Title → 2. Mission → 3. Responsibilities → 4. Qualifications → 5. Perks.

XIII

Customer Service and Retention Strategies

13.1 Retention Tactics

Loyalty Programs:
Tiered Rewards: Starbucks' "Gold Level" for frequent buyers.
Referral Bonuses: Dropbox's free storage for referrals.
Feedback Loops:
Post-purchase surveys (Typeform), NPS (Net Promoter Score) tracking.

13.2 Handling Complaints

LAFTA Method: Listen → Acknowledge → Fix → Thank → Ask for feedback.

Example: JetBlue's public apology + compensation after flight delays.

13.3 Case Study: Amazon

Obsession: Free returns, 24/7 support, Prime loyalty.
Result: 90% retention rate among Prime members.

13.4 Worksheet:

Customer Journey Audit:
Stage Touchpoints Weaknesses
Onboarding Welcome email No tutorial
13.5 Template: Service Recovery Script
1.Apologize → 2. Fix the issue → 3. Offer compensation → 4. Follow up.

XIV
Leveraging Technology and Automation

14.1 Essential Tech Stack

Productivity: Notion (project management), Slack (communication).

Marketing: HubSpot (CRM), Canva (design).

AI Tools: ChatGPT (content), Jasper (ads), DALL-E (graphics).

14.2 Automation Workflows

Sales: Zapier connects LinkedIn leads to your CRM.

Support: Chatbots (Tidio) handle 50% of FAQs.

14.3 Case Study: Shopify

• 30 •

Automation: One-click store setup, inventory syncing with suppliers.

Result: 1.7M+ merchants, $5B+ revenue.

14.4 Worksheet:

Tech Audit:
    Tool Purpose Cost
    QuickBooks Accounting $30/mo

14.5 Template: Automation Roadmap

1.Manual Task → 2. Tool → 3. Time Saved/Week.

XV
International Expansion and Global Markets

15.1 Market Entry Strategies

Localization: Adapt language, pricing (e.g., Netflix's regional content).

Partnerships: Joint ventures with local distributors (e.g., Coca-Cola in Africa).

15.2 Legal & Compliance

GDPR: Data protection for EU customers.

Taxes: VAT registration, transfer pricing rules.

15.3 Case Study: Spotify

Strategy: Launched in 178 countries with localized playlists.
Result: 500M+ users, 40% revenue from outside North America.

15.4 Worksheet:

Market Entry Checklist:
1.Research cultural norms → 2. Hire local legal counsel → 3. Test pricing.

15.5 Template: Global SWOT Analysis

Factor Strengths Weaknesses
Brand Recognition High in EU Low in Asia

XVI

Exit Strategies and Succession Planning

16.1 Exit Options

IPO: Prepare with SEC filings, investor roadshows (e.g., Snowflake's $3.4B IPO).

Acquisition: Position as a strategic fit (e.g., Instagram for Facebook's mobile growth).

16.2 Succession Planning

Family Businesses: Train successors early (e.g., Walmart's Walton family).

ESOPs: Employee Stock Ownership Plans for smooth transitions.

16.3 Case Study: WhatsApp

Journey: Sold to Facebook for $19B with 55 employees.

Lesson: "Focus on user growth, not revenue, for acquisition appeal."

16.4 Worksheet:

Exit Readiness Assessment:

Metric Score (1–10)

Financial Records 9

16.5 Template: Letter of Intent (LOI) Outline

1.Purchase Price → 2. Due Diligence Timeline → 3. Confidentiality Terms.

XVII

Bonus Strategies for Long-Term Success

1. Continuous Learning

Join mastermind groups or attend conferences (e.g., Web Summit, SXSW).

Allocate 5% of profits to team training (e.g., Coursera licenses).

2. Giving Back

1% Pledge: Donate 1% of revenue to social causes (e.g., climate action).

Mentor aspiring entrepreneurs through platforms like SCORE.

3. Personal Wellbeing

Founder Burnout Prevention:
Delegate tasks → Schedule "no work" days → Practice mindfulness.

4. Legacy Building

Document your journey (e.g., write a memoir or host a podcast).
Build a succession plan to ensure business continuity.

A. Templates Library

1. Business Plan Template

Executive Summary:

Mission: "To empower remote teams with AI-driven collaboration tools."

Vision: "Become the global leader in remote work solutions by 2030."

Financial Projections:

Year 1: 500Krevenue,Year2:500Krevenue,Year2:1.2M revenue, Year 3: $3M revenue.

Download Link: [Insert hyperlink to a Google Docs template].

2. Pitch Deck Template

Slide 1 (Problem): "75% of remote teams struggle with miscommunication."

Slide 5 (Traction): "1,000 active users, 20% monthly growth."

Slide 10 (Ask): "Seeking $500K for product development and marketing."

3. SOPs (Standard Operating Procedures)

Customer Onboarding SOP:

1.Send welcome email → 2. Schedule onboarding call → 3. Share tutorial videos.

Glossary of Key Terms

Burn Rate: The rate at which a company spends money (e.g., $10K/month).

MVP (Minimum Viable Product): A basic version of your product to test demand.

TAM/SAM/SOM:

TAM (Total Addressable Market): Global demand for your product.

SAM (Serviceable Addressable Market): Segment of TAM you can realistically target.

SOM (Serviceable Obtainable Market): Portion of SAM you can capture.

Tools Index

1. Market Research Tools

SEMrush: Track competitor keywords and traffic.
AnswerThePublic: Discover customer questions and pain points.

2. Financial Management

QuickBooks: Track expenses, invoices, and taxes.
Paddle: Handle global payments and subscriptions.

3. Automation

Zapier: Connect apps like Gmail, Slack, and Trello.
Make (Integromat): Advanced automation workflows.

4. Design & Branding

Canva: Create logos, social media posts, and presentations.
Figma: Collaborate on website and app designs.

RECOMMENDED READING & RESOURCES

1. Books

The Lean Startup by Eric Ries: Master rapid experimentation.

Atomic Habits by James Clear: Build routines for long-term success.

2. Podcasts

How I Built This (Guy Raz): Learn from founders like Airbnb and Spanx.

Masters of Scale (Reid Hoffman): Scaling strategies from Silicon Valley.

3. Courses

Y Combinator Startup School: Free guide to launching a startup.

Coursera Entrepreneurship Specialization: Build a business step-by-step.